Spiritual Diamonds From The Land of Worldly Wealth

An Orthodox Islamic Spirituality Perspective

EDRIS KIBALAMA

ISBN: 9798782107123

" There is a thin line between refusing to wear your coat of wisdom, and that of purposefully choosing to wrap yourself up with a flammable garment(amidst a blazing fire)"- Edris Kibalama

CONTENTS

Table of Contents

INTRODUCTION

Bismillah Arrahman Arraheem

In the name of Allah, The Entirely Merciful,

The Especially Merciful

Alhamdulillah/All praise be to Allah

The Salah and salaam on the Final Messenger

of Allah(Muhammad peace of Allah be upon

him)

To proceed:

" There is a thin line between refusing to wear your coat of wisdom, and that of purposefully choosing to wrap yourself up with a flammable garment(amidst a blazing fire)"- Edris Kibalama"

This is a book that I compiled from a deep love to share many of the spiritual gems and treasures which I have come across thus far in my continuing Journey, until we reach physical death, then The life of the grave, then Judgement day and its many events, then to either Heaven/ Paradise, or to Hellfire. May Allah guide us Ameen. May Allah give us the good of this life, the good of the next, and

May He protect us us from the punishment of

Hellfire Ameen.

May Allah guide us all Ameen

May Allah forgive me my sins and May He

pardon my mistakes

Alhamdulillah/All praise be to Allah. And the

Salah and salaam on the Final Messenger of

Allah(Muhammad peace of Allah be upon

him)

Edris Kibalama

Jumada Awwal 1443 AH

THE TEXT

1. The trick to attaining spiritual stability in

life, is to align your wants with your needs

2. Once you have aligned your wants with your needs, the doors of spiritual satisfaction and contentment make anchor within- by the will of Allah

3.Once you give without expecting reward from the people, you will experience spiritual upliftment

4. If you act mindfully(within divine principles), sooner or later, you will receive a King's welcome- In shaa Allah

5. Some of life's problems can't always be totally eliminated. Sometimes, you just have to put out preventative measures and carry out damage-mitigation

6. Do not be afraid to go through short term losses(from what most perceive) for long-term gains

7. Live by your accepted life values, don't only blurt them out

8. The one with the largest titles, in the face of critical tests, may be as intellectually

incompetent as a newly born(with few righteous exceptions)

9. Be a Location Intelligence Expert, for your own soul, so you may warn it against oncoming dangers

10. Part of wisdom is not to always say what you know

11. There is a thin line between refusing to wear your coat of wisdom, and that of purposefully choosing to wrap yourself up

with a flammable garment(amidst a blazing
fire)

12. You may have a wish or ambition to do or
achieve something, and depending on your
level of purity and closeness to Allah, He Jalla
Jalaali, may just choose to grant it to you- in
Shaa Allah

13. The spiritual battlefield is not for the
faint-hearted; it can completely incapacitate
the most intellectual of minds, cripple the
most physically strong, and ofcourse, which
trick does the Shaitaan frequently use other

than insinuating individuals, and moreso spouses to emotional warfare, eventually leading to community breakdown and general community/ social unsettlement.

Bonus Original quote for further research and contemplation- In shaa Allah

14. The amazing thing about patience is that, after many years of descending upon its seemingly inescapable/ never-ending trough, then ascending and escaping it's peak, you realise that you actually needed that lesson for your personal success.

FINAL PRAYER

May Allah increase us in beneficial knowledge. May Allah guide us, May Allah forgive us all our sins, and we ask Allah that he pardons us our shortcomings. May Allah purify our hearts and intentions, May Allah give us understanding of the religion, May Allah give us beneficial knowledge, hikmah and sincerity for His sake Alone. May Allah have Mercy and forgiveness upon us and those who preceded us.

Oh Allah guide us all Ameen

Rabbanaa, Aatinaa fiddunia hasanah, wa fil akhirati hasanah, wa qinaa 'adhabannaar

Alhamdulillah, wassalatu wassalaam 'alaa Rasuulillah

Our Lord/ Rabb, Give us the good of this world and give us the good of the afterlife and protect us from the fire of Hell Ameen

All Praises abundant and plentiful belong to Allah, and peace be upon his final Messenger Muhammad, peace and blessings be upon him, his family, his companions and all of those that follow them till the day of Judgement.

FINAL WORD

If you liked the reflective quotes, check out in the links below what was part of the fruits of this work:

1. www.edriskibalama.com

A website on creatively designed inspirational quotes images and a portfolio section outlining my achievements thus far.

2. www.muslimhomeschoolsoftware.com

A website on Home Educational Software for

children with an Islamised and Ethical

curriculum

3. www.intelligentmindsconsultancy.com

A website on IT support, WordPress

support and IT consultancy

4. www.eddykibs.com

More of my inspirational quotes merchandise

5. To contact me and see my works:

www.linkedin.com/in/edriskibalama/

6. Other published books

Search: "Edris Kibalama" on

www.amazon.co.uk

BONUS CHAPTER 1

Extracts taken from:

Reflections of an Orthodox Islamic Immigrant

1. Parable of the importance of knowledge: Know your button mushroom from a magic mushroom, as eating one is a blessing, and eating the other is a potential sin.

2. Parable on dedication: When the light refuses to switch on, use an alternative power supply.

3. Importance of travel: Sometimes, the things you wish for are not always in the locality you currently reside in.

4. Tests of Allah: It is not until you live deeply amongst the ignorant , that you would know whether you are yourself the same.

5. In a land of deep seated Jahiliyyah, I give you an advice my fellow brother or sister, never open Pandora's box even if you can physically get out eventually, the spiritual, emotional and intellectual damage to your being may never heal.

Important lesson; Never argue with an ignorant one. Don't even contemplate or think about it.

6. Always turn back to the Creator. Don't let the people's negative, abusive and derogatory words put you down. Trust in Allah, He will fulfill his promise to those who fear and trust Him alone.

7. If you are following a path that you are not meant to follow, the Creator will make it very clear to you, as long as you constantly seek His counsel. (i.e. Istikhaarah), you are sincere and you demonstrate never-ending patience (only for the sake of Allah)

BONUS CHAPTER 2

Statements on the reality of Orthodox Islamic Zuhd

1. Most poor people are not actually Zuhaad.

2. The richest man can be the greatest Zaahid than the poorest of people

3. Zuhd is a state of heart not necessarily a state of physical existence.

4. If most people knew the status of a true Zaahid (i.e. those that died in the pleasure of Allah) no one on this earth would dare to even utter a word of negativity towards them, and moreover their Creator.

5. The Zuhaad are amongst the ones that Allah chooses to be from amongst His Awliyaa and from amongst His Khaleel

6. You'd rather abuse a mushrik than even attempt to have bad intentions towards a khaleel/ walii/ sincere a'rifun/ Zaahid of Allah

7. All the Prophets were Zuhaad

BONUS CHAPTER 3

Short statement from a semi- fruitarian, ethical living Advocate and a World change proponent through self-rectifying Activism:

One fruit a day keeps the Doctor away,

Five fruits a day keeps the Physician at bay,

Ten fruits a day puts the Surgeon in disarray.

And adding plant based, whole grain foods,

alludes to the unethical, malady- inducing

entities of perpetrating Bio-medical and

Health- Endangering downplay

-Edris Kibalama

#semifruitarian #semivegan #flexitarian

#edriskibalama #plantbased #healthyeating

#healthyeatinghabits #Fruits #health

#healthyfood #healthiswealth

#healthylifestyle #changetheworld

#personalchange #smallchangesbigresults

#smallchanges #smallchangesbigimpact

#smallchangesmakeabigdifference

#socialchange #youarethechange #ethical

#ethicalliving #ethicallifestyle

#personalchange #SelfRectification

#selfactivism